The Lord's Prayer

By
Albert Hay Malotte

String Quartet
(Score and Parts)

Arranged by John Moss

ED-3983

ISBN 978-0-7935-4538-4

G. SCHIRMER, Inc.

DISTRIBUTED BY

HAL•LEONARD®
CORPORATION

7777 W. BLUEMOUND RD. P.O. BOX 13819 MILWAUKEE, WI 53213

THE LORD'S PRAYER

Albert Hay Malotte
arranged by John Moss

THE LORD'S PRAYER

VIOLIN 1

Albert Hay Malotte
arranged by John Moss

THE LORD'S PRAYER

VIOLIN 2

Albert Hay Malotte
arranged by John Moss

THE LORD'S PRAYER

VIOLA

Albert Hay Malotte
arranged by John Moss

THE LORD'S PRAYER

CELLO

Albert Hay Malotte
arranged by John Moss